MW01282370

Notebook

To

Happy Birthday

With love and best wishes from:

Photo credits: Ivan Busatt, Konrad-Adenauer-Stiftung, Pfan70,
Clinton Groves, Fast Fission, Georges Jansoone
© Montpelier Publishing, London 2018

1949 Birthday Notebook

◇◇

1 January
The Indo-Pakistani war ends in a stalemate and the division of Kashmir.

1949 Birthday Notebook

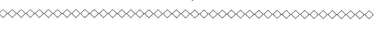

1 January
Peacetime military conscription (National Service) comes
into force in Great Britain, for men aged 18-26.

◇◇

17 January

The first post-war Volkswagen Type One (known as the Beetle or Bug) arrives in the USA. Only two are sold in 1949.

1949 Birthday Notebook

◇◇

20 January
Harry S Truman is sworn in for his first full term as US President.

1949 Birthday Notebook

25 January
The first Emmy Awards (the TV version of the Oscars) are presented in Hollywood.

1949 Birthday Notebook

<><><><><><><><><><><><><><><><><><><><><><><><><><><><><><><><><><>

25 January
David Ben-Gurion becomes the first Prime Minister of
Israel.

1949 Birthday Notebook

26 January
Australians, formerly classed as British subjects, receive separate status as Australian citizens.

1949 Birthday Notebook

31 January
Chinese communist forces enter Peking (Beijing).

1949 Birthday Notebook

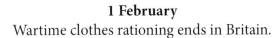

1 February
Wartime clothes rationing ends in Britain.

10 February

Arthur Miller's tragedy *Death of a Salesman* opens in New York. It runs for 742 performances.

28 February
Margaret Roberts (later Thatcher) is appointed the
Conservative party candidate for Dartford, Kent.

1 March
World heavyweight boxing champion Joe Louis retires.

1949 Birthday Notebook

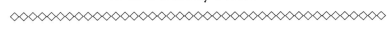

2 March
The USAF B-50 bomber *Lucky Lady II* completes the first non-stop round the world flight, with mid-air refueling.

1949 Birthday Notebook

24 March
Hamlet, starring Laurence Olivier, wins Best Picture at the
21st Academy Awards.

28 March

British astronomer Fred Hoyle coins the term 'big bang' to describe the origin of the universe.

◇◇

31 March
The British colony of Newfoundland becomes part of
Canada.

1949 Birthday Notebook

◇◇

1 April
The Marquess of Bath opens Longleat House to tourists, the first privately owned historic house to do so.

◇◇

4 April
The North Atlantic Treaty is signed, creating the NATO defence alliance.

◇◇

7 April

The musical *South Pacific* by Rodgers and Hammerstein, becomes an immediate success after opening on Broadway.

18 April
Southern Ireland is officially declared a Republic and leaves the British Commonwealth.

18 April

British comedian Will Hay (*Oh Mr Porter, Ask a Policeman*) dies aged 60.

_____

_____

_____

_____

_____

_____

_____

_____

_____

_____

_____

_____

_____

_____

◇◇

20 April

The Yangtse Incident: the Royal Navy ship HMS Amethyst, sent to evacuate British citizens from China, is held captive by communist forces until it manages to escape on 20 July.

◇◇

24 April

Wartime rationing of sweets ends in Britain but is soon reinstated due to shortages, and not finally ended until 1953.

1949 Birthday Notebook

◇◇

26 April
The Ealing Comedy film *Passport to Pimlico* is released in
the UK.

◇◇

28 April

The British Commonwealth is renamed 'The Commonwealth of Nations', with India and other republics permitted to retain membership.

_____

_____

_____

_____

_____

_____

_____

_____

_____

_____

_____

_____

_____

_____

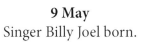

9 May
Singer Billy Joel born.

◇◇◇

11 May
Siam is officially renamed Thailand.

12 May

The Soviet Union lifts its blockade of the allied occupied
sections of Berlin, in place since 24 June 1948.

1949 Birthday Notebook

26 May
British politician and Leader of Her Majesty's Opposition
Jeremy Corbyn born.

_____

_____

_____

_____

_____

_____

_____

_____

_____

_____

_____

_____

_____

_____

1949 Birthday Notebook

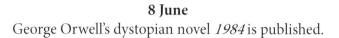

8 June
George Orwell's dystopian novel *1984* is published.

14 June
A rhesus monkey named Albert II becomes the first primate to enter space, in a modified V2 rocket.

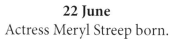

22 June
Actress Meryl Streep born.

◇◇

24 June
The first TV western, *Hopalong Cassidy*, airs on NBC in the USA.

1949 Birthday Notebook

29 June

The government of South Africa bans mixed marriage.

◇◇◇

11 July
German ship *Pamir* becomes the last commercial sailing ship to round Cape Horn.

1949 Birthday Notebook

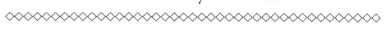

20 July
Israel and Syria sign a truce, ending the 19 month long war between them.

◇◇◇

27 July
The prototype commercial jet airliner, the de Havilland Comet, makes its first test flight.

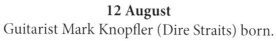

12 August
Guitarist Mark Knopfler (Dire Straits) born.

16 August
Novelist Margaret Mitchell, author of *Gone With the Wind,*
dies aged 48.

1949 Birthday Notebook

21 August
Bones thought to be of the first Pope, the Apostle Peter, are found under the Vatican in Rome.

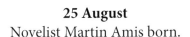

25 August
Novelist Martin Amis born.

1949 Birthday Notebook

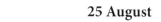

25 August
Rock musician Gene Simmons of Kiss born.

29 August
The Council of Europe meets for the first time.

1949 Birthday Notebook

29 August
The Soviet Union tests its first atomic bomb,
codenamed 'Joe 1'.

1949 Birthday Notebook

31 August
Allied-backed nationalist forces achieve victory over communists in Greece, ending the country's civil war.

1949 Birthday Notebook

31 August
Actor Richard Gere born.

2 September
The Cold War thriller *The Third Man*, starring Trevor
Howard and Orson Welles, is released in the UK. The film
wins the Grand Prix at the Cannes Film festival.

◇◇

6 September

Howard Unruh kills thirteen of his neighbours in Camden, New Jersey, in America's first single episode mass murder.

◇◇

7 September
The allied military government of west Germany gives way
to the Federal Republic of Germany under Konrad Adenaur.

1949 Birthday Notebook

19 September
The British Pound Sterling is devalued from $4.03 to $2.80.

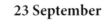

23 September
Rock musician Bruce Springsteen born.

◇◇

29 September

Iva Toguri D'Aquino, thought to be the wartime pro-Japanese broadcaster 'Tokyo Rose', is convicted of treason. This is later overturned due to lack of evidence.

◇◇◇

1 October

The People's Republic of China is officially proclaimed, and recognised by the Soviet Union on 2 October.

7 October

The German Democratic Republic (East Germany) is established.

1949 Birthday Notebook

15 November
Nathuram Godse and Narayan Apte are executed for the
assassination of Mahatma Gandhi in 1948.

◇◇

8 December

The capitalist Chinese government-in-exile, ousted by the communist uprising, retreats to Taiwan and declares Taipei as its capital.

1949 Birthday Notebook

13 December
The Israeli parliament votes to move its capital to Jerusalem.

◇◇

15 December
Actor Don Johnson (*Miami Vice*) born.

27 December
Queen Juliana of the Netherlands grants sovereignty to the
Dutch colony of Indonesia.

_____

_____

_____

_____

_____

_____

_____

_____

_____

_____

_____

_____

_____

_____

_____

41575893R00035

Made in the USA
Lexington, KY
08 June 2019